# RED CLAY

## Poems & Stories

# RED CLAY

## Poems & Stories
## Linda Hogan

The Greenfield Review Press
Greenfield Center, NY

The poems and stories in this book are a compilation of the work
which appeared in two previous volumes: *Calling Myself Home*
(Greenfield Review Press 1978) and *That Horse* (Pueblo of Acoma
Press 1985).

Publication of this book has been made possible, in part, through a
Literary Publishing grant from the Literature Program of the New
York State Council on the Arts.

ISBN 0-912678-83-6

Library of Congress #91-76640

Distribution by
The Talman Co., Inc.
131 Spring Street
New York, NY 10012
(212) 431-7175     FAX (212) 431-7215

Composition by Sans Serif, Ann Arbor, Mi. 48104
Printed in the United States of America

Cover Art by Marilyn Auer

# CONTENTS

## CALLING MYSELF HOME

## THAT HORSE

For my mother whose body brought forth mine.
For my father whose words kept me going.
For all those who came before us.
For those who come after.
For all their stories.

# CALLING MYSELF HOME

# INTRODUCTION

1991

For American Indian people the journey home is what tells us our human history, the mystery of our lives here, and leads us toward fullness and strength. These first poems were part of that return for me, an identification with my tribe and the Oklahoma earth, a deep knowing and telling how I was formed of these two powers called ancestors and clay.

These poems grew out of the Oklahoma terrain resonant with the calls of frogs, my grandfather's horse and wagon, my grandmother's uncut braids worn wrapped about her head in the traditional Chickasaw manner, the firefly-lit nights we sat outside and heard stories, including the one of the gunstocks made from our stolen black walnut trees. In these poems live red land and light.

Our story, of which I am only a small part, is a history both of Oklahoma's Indian Territory and of the hard road of political betrayal that led us there and that led some of us to other lands, places where our uprooted lives have felt broken. It is also the story of an incredible will of survival, how some of us fell through history alive.

The desperate need to articulate this was what went into these early poems, the need to say what hadn't been spoken, to tell an untold story of our lives. They are home speaking through me. Home is in blood, and I am still on the journey of calling myself home.

# BY THE DRY POND

*These poems were written for my sister, Donna*

# TURTLE

I'm dreaming the old turtle back.
He walks out of water,
slow,
that shell with water on it
sun on it,
dark as the wet trunks of hackberry trees.

In water
the world is breathing,
in the silt.
There are fish
and their blood changes easy
warm to cold.

And the turtle,
small yellow bones of animals inside
are waking
to shine out from his eyes.
Wake up the locusts whose dry skins
are still sleeping on the trees.

We should open his soft parts,
pull his shells apart
and wear them on our backs
like old women who can see the years
back through his eyes.

Something is breathing in there.
Wake up, we are women.
The shells are on our backs.
We are amber,
the small animals
are gold inside us.

# HACKBERRY TREES

We walk small
over the dry pond,
old bowl of earth.
We walk over the fine bones of fish
buried in powdered silt
beside hooks.

This summer the turtle is gone,
pupil in the eye we called water
that watched us grow dry.

The trees are all that's left of water.
Beneath them the crickets
are sawing their legs
dust for rosin.
Turn up a stone and they keep silent.

On the dark trunks of trees
shells of bronze insects
are open at the back.

We are like the trees,
they have been in this place so long
their yellow hearts could open.
The insects walk over our warm skin.
They think we are the earth.

# RED CLAY

Turtle, old as earth
his slow neck has pushed aside
to bury him for winter.

His heart beats slow.
And the fish
are embedded in ice.

I photograph you
at the potter's wheel, the light
and the dark of you.

Tonight the turtle is growing
a larger shell, calcium
from inside sleep.

The moon grows
layer on layer
across iced black water.

On the clay your fingertips
are wearing away
the red soil.

We are here, the red earth
passes like light into us
and stays.

# CALLING MYSELF HOME

There were old women
who lived on amber.
Their dark hands
laced the shells of turtles
together, pebbles inside
and they danced
with rattles strong on their legs.

There is a dry river
between them and us.
Its banks divide up our land.
Its bed was the road
I walked to return.

We are plodding creatures
like the turtle
born of an old people.
We are nearly stone
turning slow as the earth.
Our mountains are underground
they are so old.

This land is the house
we have always lived in.
The women,
their bones are holding up the earth.
The red tail of a hawk
cuts open the sky
and the sun
brings their faces back
with the new grass.

Dust from yarrow
is in the air,
the yellow sun.
Insects are clicking again.

I came back to say good-bye
to the turtle
to those bones
to the shells locked together
on his back,
gold atoms dancing underground.

# FINDING BEADS

White beads,
we strung them together with fish line
clear as water.
And the beads,
small bones of birds,
rattled around our necks
while we dug more earth
from the dried pond.

Such clouds that could have risen
in formations, flying up
to put flesh back on the birds,
red organs drumming inside.
Bones which let air travel,
their absence left holes in the sky.

Beads made of bone, our vertebrae,
arms and legs
strung together beneath skin,
our own bones still fitting
mortar and pestle.
Our hands like the dry reeds
knotted together
could sweep all this away,
break the clear thread.

## GOING TO TOWN

I wake up early while you sleep,
soft in that room whose walls
are pictures of blonde angels,
and set loose the fireflies.
Their lights
have flickered all night
on our eyelids.

Already you have a woman's hip bones,
long muscles
you slide your dress over
and we brush each other's hair
then step out into the blue morning.
Good daughters,
we are quiet
lifting empty milk cans,
silver cans into the wagon.
They rattle together
going to town.

We ride silent
because the old man has paid us
dimes not to speak
but the wheels of the wagon
sing and we listen,
we listen to ourselves singing
the silence of birds
and dust that flies up in our hair.

The dust moves closer to us,
the place is dark
where we have disappeared.
Our family returns to us
in the bodies of children, of dogs
stretched across the road,
cats who ran away from home.

What do we have left
except the mirage of sound,
frogs creaking over the night land.
The black walnut trees are gone,
stolen during the night
and transformed
into the handles of guns.

That song, if you sing for it
and pray it to come,
in the distance
it grows nearer.
Close your eyes and it comes,
the music of old roads
we still travel together, so far
the sound is all that can find us.

## STOLEN TREES

The sound we make sleeping,
quiet, the trees at night
stolen by the dark silhouettes of men.
Such a strange peace,
the empty sky.
And the men so quietly moved
black walnut trunks
to the edge of the world,
transformed dark wood
into the sleek handles of rifles.

Where they were
the air is thin.
The rain,
I could climb it up to the sky.
Vacant places where the dark
vertebraes of trees
pushed sugar
rising up from trunks.
They held crows
in their branches
feathers scorched black.
The wings took shape
in the air around us.
Trees whose wood flash
light. Trees, beautiful trees
who can kill a man
like the fallen wings of crows.

# CROWS

Hear them speak like men
to one another. Their gravel voices
are thunder breaking the sky,
a gun cracking air,
the bad air
filled with birds whose wings
tip indigo in the light.

Beneath them, men with blue guns
turn up the whites of their eyes.
The feathers,
the feathers come apart, falling
specks of dust.

My ears want to hear them
begin to speak,
to hear the dark berries
uncoil through flesh.
They are quiet,
so still
I wait for a breath
to escape the warm feathers.

# REMEMBERING THE LIGHTNING

In that flash of light
our faces are shiny, silver
as the new silver dollars
in grandpa's cold pockets.

At the dark window
we breathe each other's hair,
warm skin.
Blue,
female thighs
beneath the hems of our slips.

Silver light down the dark sky
stops the man we love
and fear between heartbeats.
It's dark.
The place where he stood
is empty with night.
Behind the fences,
nitrogen and oxygen
are splitting apart.

And we remember him,
a blur of flesh
moving in starts across the slow field,
his dark hand
brushing light
out of the fur of an enchanted horse.

The sky crackles like a gun
and shadows of thin trees
fall down to the ground.

# CELEBRATION: BIRTH OF A COLT

When we reach the field
she is still eating
the heads of yellow flowers
and pollen has turned her whiskers
gold. Lady,
her stomach bulges out,
the ribs have grown wide.
We wait,
our bare feet dangling
in the horse trough,
warm water
where goldfish brush
our smooth ankles.
We wait
while the liquid breaks
down Lady's dark legs
and that slick wet colt
like a black tadpole
darts out
beginning at once
to sprout legs.
She licks it to its feet,
the membrane still there,
red,
transparent
the sun coming up shines through,
the sky turns bright with morning
and the land
with pollen blowing off the corn,
land that will always own us,
everywhere it is red.

# HERITAGE

# NATIVITY

Old women
fire clay ovens.
There will be bread.

Six men
work on the church
lifting the cross.
The day is heat.

Lower your head
through the many eyes
that burn into flesh
and beyond.

White sun.
There are no shadows.
In the center of dust
a bridge crosses brief water.

A child stares into my face,
my eyes.
Guilty, I smile.

Bread.
The smell
comes from stone.

# HERITAGE

From my mother, the antique mirror
where I watch my face take on her lines.
She left me the smell of baking bread
to warm fine hairs in my nostrils,
she left the large white breasts that weigh down
my body.

From my father I take his brown eyes,
the plague of locusts that leveled our crops,
they flew in formation like buzzards.

From my uncle the whittled wood
that rattles like bones
and is white
and smells like all our old houses
that are no longer there. He was the man
who sang old chants to me, the words
my father was told not to remember.

From my grandfather who never spoke
I learned to fear silence.
I learned to kill a snake
when begging for rain.

And grandmother, blue-eyed woman
whose skin was brown,
she used snuff.
When her coffee can full of black saliva
spilled on me
it was like the brown cloud of grasshoppers
that leveled her fields.
It was the brown stain
that covered my white shirt.
That sweet black liquid like the food
she chewed up and spit into my father's mouth
when he was an infant.

It was the brown earth of Oklahoma
stained with oil.
She said tobacco would purge your body of poisons.
It has more medicine than stones and knives
against your enemies.
That tobacco is the dark night that covers me.

She said it is wise to eat the flesh of deer
so you will be swift and travel over many miles.
She told me how our tribe has always followed a stick
that pointed west
that pointed east.
From my family I have learned the secrets
of never having a home.

# THANKSGIVING

Turkey, blue head on the ground
body in a gleaming white tub
with lion claw feet.
Heat rises in the yard
melting crystals of ice
and there are feathers, bronze,
metallic blue and green
that were his strong wings
which never flew away.

And we give thanks for it
and for the old woman
shawl pulled tight around her
she sits
her teeth brown
her body dry
her spoons
don't match.

Some geese, last stragglers
trickling out of Canada
are flying over.
Noisy, breaking the glass sky
grey
they are grey
and their wings are weightless.

# MAN IN THE MOON

He's the man who climbs his barn
to look down on the fields,
the man leading his horse from the barn
that finally fell down.

When I'm quiet he speaks:
we're like the spider
we weave new beds around us
when old ones are swept away.

When I see too much
I follow his advice
and close my worn-out eye.

Yesterday he was poor
but tomorrow he says his house
will fill up with silver
the white flesh will fatten on his frame.

Old man, window in a sky
full of holes
I am like you
putting on a new white shirt
to drive away on the fine roads.

# FISHERMAN

The sun, yellow spider,
climbs the sky and lets down
its web of dust.

Old man at the horizon,
he's on top of the world
blowing smoke.

His fish basket is empty
except for the lures
in their nest of clear thread.

Under water a fish,
Old Whiskers they call him
breaks away.

Sunlight and air
pulled in on a line.

# ARROWHEAD

I hear the soft breath
of horses,
ghosts resting in heat,
the muffled hooves
turning from the sun.

Here
where the smell of pine is thick,
I rest beneath this tree
holding broken flint.

Eyes closed,
I see a woman grinding corn
in a round stone basin
and soft feet hit earth
dry as the air.

In the breeze
are the sounds of this man
chipping stone,
his old knees bent
and birds
falling
down his mind.

# LEAVING

Good-bye, divisions of people:
      those hickory-chopping,
      the hump hunters,
      skunk people
      dung people
      people who live under trees
      who live in broken houses
      and parts of houses.
      Their house worn out people
      are the meanest of all.

My house-cut-off people, I'm saying good-bye
to that person behind me.
She's the one
who tried to please her father,
the one an uncle loved for her dark hair.

White coyote behind me
light up your eyes, your white shadows,
your white round mouth
in its cage of black trees, a moon
running from branch to branch.
Moon that lives in the water,
snapping turtle that crawled out
at me.

Good-bye shooting horse
      above a dead man's grave.
Let that blessed rain
where fish descended from the sky
                evaporate.

Silver lures, minnows
in that river who is the moon
living in a broken house,
who is the coyote

dwelling among the blackjack broken off
people, the turtle
who lives in its round white shell,
            I can tell you good-bye.

Good-bye to the carved bone beads
I found by the river. They can grow back
their flesh,
        their small beating hearts,
        air in the bones
        and gray wings they fly
        away from me.

Good-bye to the milky way
        who lives in his old worn out place,
        dog white
        his trail.

All my people are weeping
when I step out of my old skin
like a locust singing good-bye,
feet still clinging
to the black walnut tree.
They say I've burned all my brown sticks
for telling time
and still it passes away.

# COYOTE

Steel jaws are tense to clamp shut.
The man is leaving,
the small coyote comes sniffing
soft, soft
feathers from the sky go out quiet like wings.

Such fragile things we all are,
such bones,
such silk nests of hair, fine nerves
touching the smooth beads of vertebrae
that string us together.
Coyote with invisible breath
calling for snow and wind.

Now the evergreen is turning slowly
from your eyes. Something, a bird,
goes up in the air.

Coyote, you weren't much,
nothing more than a shadow with eyes,
a wisp of air waiting to leave
through the thin bones.

All of us have stolen something
in the night
the long night ending in sweat,
the blackest sweat
the morning on the ground.

# AFTER FISH

Between gills
I stabbed the knife
spilling eggs from catfish bellies
masses of pearl
emptied before eyes
going cold.
The cats come from nowhere
come on the road of fish smell
and they are as strange in this dry place
as tulips growing among dead weeds.

The sun bakes and bleaches the land
fish belly white.
Night is a blessing
and the moon passes over thirsty ground
like a star over fire.

The fish are gone now
driven by summer,
having worked their silver bodies
into mud, caked
and waiting for rain.

Hooked on old habits
and seeing the moon
float by in daylight,
I catch the knife
and slit the pale crescent.
Its bowels trail down.
The sun beats with blades of fire
glinting over metal.
The heat throbs my temples.
The cats come from nowhere.

# BLESSING

Blessed
are the injured animals
for they live in his cages.
But who will heal my father,
tape his old legs for him?

Here's his bird with the two broken wings
and her feathers are white as an angel
and she says goddamn stirring grains
in the kitchen. When the birds fly out
he leaves the cages open
and she kisses his brow for such
good works.

    Work he says
    all your damned life
    and at the end
    you don't own even a piece of land.

Blessed are the rich
for they eat meat every night.
They have already inherited the earth.

For the rest of us, may we just live
long enough
and unwrinkle our brows,
may we keep our good looks
and some of our teeth
and our bowels regular.

Perhaps we can go live in places
a rich man can't inhabit,
in the sunfish and jackrabbits,
in the cinnamon colored soil,
the land of red grass
and red people

in the valley
of the shadow of Elk
who aren't there.

    He says the old earth
    wobbles so hard, you'd best hang on
    to everything. Your neighbors
    steal what little you got.

Blessed are the rich
for they don't have the same old
Everyday to put up with
like my father
who's gotten old,
        Chickasaw
        chikkih asachi, which means
they left as a tribe not a very great while ago.
They are always leaving, those people.

Blessed
are those who listen
when no one is left to speak.

# LEFT HAND CANYON

"Remember what Chief Left Hand said?
Never mind. Everything else
was taken from him
let's leave his grief alone."
                    William Matthews

In the air
which moves the grass
moves the fur of a black horse
his words come back,
the old griefs
carried on the wind.

Left Hand returns to speak,
wind in the blood of those
who will listen.
If his words were taken from him,
I'm giving them back.
These words,
if you listen
they are real.
These words,
a hand has written them.

Everything speaks.
Put your ear to the earth
and hear it, the trees speaking,
mining for minerals.

You can't take a man's words.
They are his even as the land
is taken away
where another man
builds his house.

And the night animals,
their yellow eyes
give back the words
while you are sleeping
when all the old animals
come back
from their secret houses
of air.

# MOSQUITOES

To keep them from you,
paint yourself
red as the natives.
They will not drink
blood exposed to air
only pure blood
embedded deep in flesh.

If you hate them
hum D minor, the breeding song.
They will be drawn to you,
forgetting to mate
and loving only the sound
of your voice.

Or when one lands
drinking at the rivers of your arm,
make a fist, clenched
and pulsing blood into the thin needle
of mosquito until it swells
with your life and bursts
red into air.

I will not sleep with nets,
burn a yellow light
or citron candle.
When one hums silently
around my ears,
bends its knees upon my arm,
I will be still as a stone
at the edge of water,
watching my blood carried into air.

# THE RIVER CALLS THEM

Tadpoles in a jar
a shock of legs sprouted
tail swallowed into
bones growing from nothing,
dark nipples of
toes creeping out,
one at a time.
And the sudden need for mud.

Puffed throats and night
signals young hunters
and frogs are bathed in the salt
of child hands,
moist skin dried in too much sun,
starved beside a heap of dead flies.

At funerals
their eyes are gold
summer gazing at land,
cold toes turned into twigs.
Stiff frogs are dropped into earth
damp and waiting.

# RAIN

When it rains fish
we say
night's bird is shaking out her wings.

It's morning and the children
in loose cotton pajamas
let screen doors slam behind them.
Bare feet are slipping,
clear scales and roe
pressed into pavement.
Rusty pails fill up.

The cast iron skillet
hisses with oil
and corn meal pops.
White stomachs,
rainbow flecks of skin.

In the streets
the sun dries fish into silver lures,
sun that brings fish,
children and even the rain
back home again.

# SONG FOR MY NAME

Before sunrise
think of brushing out an old woman's
dark braids.
Think of your hands,
fingertips on the soft hair.

If you have this name,
your grandfather's dark hands
lead horses toward the wagon
and a cloud of dust follows,
ghost of silence.

That name is full of women
with black hair
and men with eyes like night.
It means no money
tomorrow.

Such a name my mother loves
while she works gently
in the small house.
She is a white dove
and in her own land
the mornings are pale,
birds sing into the white curtains
and show off their soft breasts.

If you have a name like this,
there's never enough water.
There is too much heat.
When lightning strikes, rain
refuses to follow.
It's my name,
that of a woman living
between the white moon
and the red sun, waiting to leave.

It's the name that goes with me
back to earth
no one else can touch.

# VAPOR CAVE

Daughter of stones,
my body that looks like a woman
is hard underneath.
Hipbones in their sharp crescent
are moving aside.
Beneath my white feet
the ground is hot.
Steam rises out of the land.
My body letting go
everything goes out, my eyes,
my ears, old voices.
Steam water,
smoke from the earth,
hot springs under the stone
enter the soles of my feet.
Keep me free from sickness.
Enter the path of my veins
my children
my seeds.
Legs and arms lose themselves
lose their light boundaries of skin.
Old voices,
I think I hear them
speaking
up the long stairway of my back,
white steps
toward the sounds of air.
The sun is bright.
The sky is clear.
Each tip of the grass is shining.

# INTRODUCTION

## *My Father's Story: The Black Horse*

My father's stories sometimes crop up in my work. They become pieces of the written story like a finger that points the way, or a leg that helps the story to walk. Sometimes they are the heart, giving the writing its oxygen and blood.

He wrote down the story of the black horse and turned it over to me. I suspect it was to make sure that I got it right at least once, because I not only fictionalize, but I have my own memory of the stories and how I heard them, and my own version of the truth.

I no longer think of my writing as "telling the truth." Adhering only to facts limits the work, and I wonder if truth-telling is possible, given how human perception works. Writing is a way to uncover and discover a new truth. It comes from, and speaks to, the deepest well-spring of the human being, the place that is the source of our inner knowledge, intuition and instinct. Fiction clarifies the world without muddling life with the bias of fact.

"The Black Horse," in my father's style, is wonderful and rich in texture. He thought I would "fix" it for him. I felt it was whole in itself, but I had been wanting to write about Shorty for years. I wrote several drafts of a poem about that horse; not one of the versions worked. For months I looked at my father's story. When my father wrote of grandfather falling, drunk, off the horse and how the horse stayed with him, I remember my grandfather riding in one night during an Oklahoma lightning storm. I watched, afraid, from the window. Years later, the incident became a poem in my first book:

> Silver light down the dark sky
> stops the man we love
> and fear between heartbeats.

It's dark.
The place where he stood
is empty with night.
Behind the fences,
nitrogen and oxygen
are splitting apart.
                    (from "Remembering the Lightning")

I remembered, also, reading my father's story, how my father broke and trained horses later at a ranch south of Colorado Springs, and how he put me on their backs as extra weight. When he wrote of bronc riding, I pictured all the rodeos we attended, Casey Tibbs, girls in gold lamé western pants, my Uncle Jake who is a ferrier and specializes in rodeo horses.

My dad mentioned Nathan Woodward, the man who married my Aunt Louise, grew cotton and winter wheat, who told me once about the death of my grandfather's red mules and land loss during the depression. Last summer my youngest daughter and I visited his grave, walking through a long and dark corridor of cedars to the cemetery in Martha, Oklahoma.

In my memory, also, I could see my father studying math and English. I pictured Will as that student. He is at least half my father. And hearing the men speak Chickasaw has turned through my bones all my life. I knew there was something here that I wanted to write. I laid aside my father's story in order to get close to what I wanted to say. What I noticed about "The Black Horse," his story, was that at the end there was a difference in what my father said and what I had heard in the past. For instance, I know that things were not too good for Indians in the territory. The time was right after the oil boom which resulted in loss of Indian lives and land. It was right after statehood, which my Chickasaw grandparents never acknowledged. It was just prior to the Depression. And the majority of Indian Territory stories were violent and fearful ones; it was my father who told me about the night riders coming by and his father concealing a gun as he walked out of the house to meet the men on horses.

The allotment where my father lived as a boy is now the Ardmore Airport. I have heard how it once looked, where the black pasture was, the water. But I created the story around the land I remembered from childhood and family visits. I added the history I remembered from some reading, an incident related to me by Carol Hunter, an Osage scholar of that time period. I added the illegal timber industry that partially created the dustbowl. I added my cousin Coy Colbert and his maps of our lands that are currently leased with no payment to the tribe. The story grows to become a story of Indian life and land.

"That Horse," in my version, is mostly fiction based on history, on my father's stories, on my own experience. I had to let my father's story go in order to write it. His story is his. My story is mine. My grandfather would have another way of telling. Together we created an illustration of how the oral becomes the written, how life becomes a story, how new angles and layers of information create a form of energy that lets the story enter.

It was through my father's imagination that the writer in me was nourished. As a girl, when I got things wrong, he never corrected me or made me feel small. There was no harm in letting me go around with a head full of so-called imagination. He often said, "You're probably right, Linda." I am grateful for that gift.

Just after I finished this story, I was driving my truck into town. My daughter, Tanya, was talking with me while we drove. We drove past a field where we had seen many coyotes. Passing the field, I thought of our dog that disappeared last summer. I said, "Wouldn't it be something if Annie was out here living with the coyotes?" Tanya said, "She probably is. After all, she is half coyote." Annie was an Australian cattle dog, but I didn't tell my daughter. After all, she may want to write stories some day. Besides, Annie *did* have a coyote tail and those big coyote ears.

I said, "I think you're right, Tanya."

# THE BLACK HORSE

The horse traders used to come by, in a wagon and leading the horses behind the wagon. Some of them would be riding a horse or driving them. They would go around the country and trade horses or anything else they might have.

If they had a horse you thought might be better than yours then you and the horse trader would start to talking trade. Sometimes it would take a day or two to make the trade, and this was because he would always want something else. That was called "Boot". It would usually be money. He might say that he would trade his horse for yours if you gave him $25.00 to boot, maybe less or maybe more. It always turned out that he would want something for that was the way he made his living.

One day a horse trader came by our house and had several horses he wanted to trade. We always had several horses in the horse lot. This time my dad didn't want to trade, so they just talked and the horse trader had dinner with us, for my dad had known him for a long time. He was leading a little colt behind the wagon, and after a while of talking and visiting they went out to the wagon. This man did not want to lead this young horse around the country, because he was about a year old and it wasn't good for him to be exerted that much.

He wanted money for the colt, and they bartered for quite sometime. Then dad went to the horse lot and caught a horse and lead him out. He was tied to the wagon and the little black horse was untied and led to the barn. He was not put with the other horses. Instead he was put in a stall and fed oats and hay. He was given special treatment from that day on. When he put on some weight he was the blackest horse I ever saw and was slick and shiny like silver. He flashed in the sun when he ran around the lot. He was not ever let out with the other horses in the pasture. He stayed in the barn except when dad took him out for water and walked him around the place. He got gentle and was brushed often to keep his coat shiny.

He was something special to my dad, and he wouldn't let us kids have anything to do with him like we did with the other horses. He was my dad's horse and we all knew it. We rode all the other horses and fed and watered them and used them like all animals were used on the farm. If we wanted to go to the other end of the farm, or take water to the working hands, we would just jump on a horse and carry the water to them. I was small but we had a stump that we would get on and from there we could get on the horse with ease.

Shorty grew into a very good animal, however he was not as large as most of the horses on the ranch. He was stocky and strong. He was quite fast for a short distance. He stood out in the presence of other horses. When he was about three years old, my dad began his training. With a rope and a halter he was being taught to lead and to react to the halter (called Halter Broke) and he got to the point where he would just follow my dad all around the horse lot and all over the place. He was very gentle and never kicked or objected to any of the kids petting him. They could walk under him and he would stand perfectly still, as if he were afraid of hurting one of them. That was quite different from the way the other horses acted. They did not want anyone bothering them. So, all the kids liked Shorty very well.

When it came time to break Shorty to ride, we all thought that would be a good show. Although dad had put the saddle on him several times before then and let him walk around for some time with it on and he didn't object, like most young horses do. They usually Buck and Pitch a lot when first ridden. In fact, it took a good bronc rider to ride some of them. My oldest brother Rip was a good rider and could ride bronc horses very well. He was no match for my dad. He was as good a bronc rider as there was in that country at that time. He was also the best horse trainer in the country.

The time came to ride Shorty. My dad saddled him and lead him out to a lot that was vacant of any animals. We all gathered on the fence to watch. I mean all: mother, my sisters, and us boys. Well, we were somewhat disappointed I guess, for we were expecting to see a good bronc riding show. My dad put on his spurs, pulled down his hat so it wouldn't blow off, pulled Shorty's head around to the mounting side and held it while he put his boot in the stirrup and gracefully swung on top of the horse and settled in the saddle ready for the worst.

He was surprised, for when he turned Shorty's head loose, Shorty just looked around and started walking around the lot. Dad would rein him in all directions around the lot and started him to trotting and then into a gallop; and the horse obeyed as if he had done this all of his life. He never did buck and was very smart and learned all there was to learn in record time. It wasn't long until he was a good roping horse and from that day on he was my dad's working and riding horse.

I know of the time my dad drank too much when he was out checking the cattle west of the town of Berwyn. He got drunk and fell off Shorty. Well, he went to sleep and Shorty stayed with him all night, just waited until dad woke up and rode him home.

Dad was training the horse all of the time. On the weekends there was always a group of ranchers getting together and having calf and goat roping for money. They would all put in so much money for entrance fee. The one with the fastest time roping and tying an animal was the winner. It was a lot of fun and it was seldom that one cowboy would win more than once. They were all about even in this event. It would last all afternoon and everyone would have fun. There was always someone selling pop and lemonade, cookies and hotdogs.

Dad rode Shorty and he grew better all the time. Some of the ranchers would let other cowboys ride their horses to rope on, but dad would never let anyone ride Shorty except him. He would not let Rip ride him to rope off of. He was a one man horse.

Once dad rode Shorty up to the house and dropped the reins as he always did, for he knew the horse would be there when he got back. Well, I was a cowboy too; I had ridden all the gentle horses and I was at the age I thought I was pretty good and in control of everything. I went out and got on Shorty and was going to ride him. He was all right as long as we were around the horse and barn. I took him out in the pasture for a gallop. That was my mistake, for instead of just a gallop, he started to run and I could not stop him. He clamped down on the bridle and bit and it did no good for me to pull on the reins. I could ride him without any trouble. I just could not stop him. I thought about jumping off, but that was dangerous so I stayed on him, all the while trying to stop him. By the time I came by the house the first time everyone was watching. Well, my dad hollered at me to bring him by the barn and I knew he would grab the reins and stop him. I did that and when we came by, my dad could not catch the reins and we were out to another pasture. There was a pecan grove in this pasture and I decided I would run Shorty into a tree and stop him. Well, he was smarter than that. He would just go around the trees and keep on going. By this time I was beginning to panic and all I wanted to do was to get off that crazy horse.

In the meantime my dad had gone to the barn and caught the old blue horse and here he came, and guided Shorty close to him. Shorty was getting pretty tired and so was I. And dad just rode up beside us, caught the reins and stopped him. He started to lead him back to the barn, and he asked if I was all right and I said I was. Well, I knew by the way dad looked at me that I wasn't going to be so good in a little while. I said I wanted off and would walk to the barn. He told me to stay on the horse. When we got to the barn he unsaddled Shorty and took the reins to the seat of my pants. I knew I deserved the thrashing and took it like a man should.

Later on we were moving a herd of cattle from the river bottom during a flood. We had been gathering them since four in the morning. We had them all and were moving them to higher ground and dad rode up beside me and smiled at me and said, "Would you like to ride Shorty?" I knew it was supposed to be funny, but somehow it was not. I told him that I would never ride Shorty again. He laughed and rode on up the side of the cattle.

Nathan Woodward was helping us with the cattle. He smiled and said to me, "Everything is all right, Pete."

Everything was all right for we got about 400 head of cattle out of the Bottom and if we had not there would have been a lot of them drowned. It flooded for a week or so. From then on my work got harder and the hours got longer. But that is how it goes on farms and ranches. The work was hard but I never minded it.

As I looked back, I think I really liked the work. There was always something that needed to be done and there was always time to play. If we wanted to go fishing, I can't remember any time that my dad would say no. When we asked him if we could go fishing, he would say it was alright and give us a time to be back. We never failed to be back when he said, or close, for we didn't have watches and neither did he. We knew that there was work to be done and that if we did all of it we would be able to do the things we wanted to do, like fishing, hunting, swimming in the river. We had a lot of kids in the country and we were always getting together and playing games and such things that kids did.

Shorty lived a long time and died of old age.

# THAT HORSE

The dream men wore black and they were invisible except for the outlines of their bodies in the moonlight and the guns at their sides. Will walked slowly behind them until their horses turned and began to pursue him. He could not run and they had no faces in the dark.

It was early morning and his heart was pounding like the horses' hooves. The crickets were singing but there were no birds. Will pulled on his jeans and boots. Outside, mist was snaking over the land between trees and around the barn. It absorbed the sounds of morning. The rooster crowed as if from the distance.

The horse trader stood beside his wagon talking to old man Johns. He had arrived in Will's dreamtime with his horses of flesh tied behind the wagon; an older paint, a white stocky work horse, two worn-out mules, a drowsing bay, and the black colt. Will eyed them while he walked to the barn.

Will's father stood leaning against the rake as if he'd been caught hard at work. It was clear by the way he stood that he didn't want to trade.

"I been to Texas and all over." The trader removed his hat and wiped his forehead with a rag, though there was a chill in the early morning air and ghosts were flying from the breathing mouths of horses.

"Picked up that bay over there in Tishomingo."

Will stood just inside the barn, watching the men and listening.

"How's the Missus?" the trader asked as he pulled back the lips of the bay to show Mr. Johns that her teeth were not worn down.

"Just fine."

"The boys?"

Mr. Johns was not interested in the bay but he put aside the rake and helped the trader through the steps of his work, lifting her leg to examine the hoof. The horse pulled away and twitched the men's touch off her back. She knew what Will had begun to think, that a danger lies in men's hands, that whatever they touch is destroyed. She shook their bitter taste from her lips.

After the men went indoors, Will looked over the horses. He was curious about the contents of the wagon, the leather pouch alongside ropes and horse blankets, the extra saddle and burlap bag bulging with trade goods.

In the kitchen, Josie served the men thick slabs of bacon and cornbread with eggs. Will sat quietly. His brothers had gone to put up a fence at Uncle Ray's so it was a silent morning without their loud boots hitting the floor, without the young men's disordered conversation.

"I got this black colt too young to travel. Comes from real good stock."

"I got no need for a colt. It don't look too young to travel."

"You can give me that work horse out there—it's nearly broke down anyway, see the sway of its back? And give me five dollars to boot, I'll give you that colt. An Indian around here has need of a black horse."

Steam boiled from the kettle. Josie held her hands in the heat of it.

The trader continued. "Picked up that colt from that new white sheriff over in Nebo county."

"That so? Haines?"

"That's the fellow. The colt's too young to travel."

"Haven't got five dollars anyway." Will's father rubbed his chin. "All I got is dried meat."

"That'll do."

Will didn't know where the riders came from or where they were going. All that year, his father rose from his bed at night and went outdoors, his pistol concealed at his side. He exchanged words with the men who rode out of the darkness, or he fed them or gave them money, or offered them fresh horses for their journey.

Sometimes they sat around the table like bandits, all of them dressed in black, their dark horses hidden in the trees.

Or they sat on the front porch where they would not disturb Josie and the boys, or Will, who was supposed to be studying arithmetic.

The men sat with their boots up on the rail, their chairs tilted back on two legs. Will heard the words again about the sheriff, oil accidents, manhunts. Heard the whiskey bottle hit against a glass and return to the table.

About this time, a Choctaw family named Hastings who lived nearby had all disappeared except for the grandmother who was declared mentally defective. She was taken away, protesting in Indian that the sheriff and deputy had murdered her sons and daughters, and that the government officials wanted her land and the mineral rights. The sheriff who hauled her off did not understand the language she spoke. He said she was crazy as an old bear because her family had gone off to Missouri after work and jobs and left the old woman behind. The grief of it was about to kill her, he said, and she'd be better off in the hospital up in the city. But James Johns and old man Cade, a full-blood, heard the woman's words and understood. They knew she never lied and she was sane as a tree that had watched everything pass by it.

"She's crazy, all right," lied Cade to the sheriff. "Says there's ghosts on the place."

Afterwards, when they went to the hospital to talk to her, she agreed to stay there until it was safe to return to her allotment land. They didn't tell her that the land was already torn up and that it spit blue flames into the night from the oil works and that the small pond she had loved was filled in with earth.

In the hills there were bodies of Indians, most of them wrapped in blankets, the smell of whiskey on the clothing of even those who were known teetotalers and Baptists.

Mr. Johns' face hardened, but he set to work. His routine included brushing the horse, Shorty, until the black fur was like water reflecting the sun. He kept him separate from the other horses as if they would give the men's secrets away to that one who had been owned by Sheriff Haines. The horse heard only the voice of James Johns. As it grew, it was enchanted by the man's voice and tales. Mr. Johns allowed no one else near the black horse.

He grew muscular, that horse, and his stamping hooves shook the ground.

One day the Indian agent arrived at the door. Mr. Johns said to Will, "Don't you ever forget that the only goal of white men is to make money." And he went out like he had nothing but time and stood on the front porch and looked squarely into the agent's face.

The young man was fair-haired, like cornsilk, and had flushed cheekbones. He gave a paper to Mr. Johns, "You are good honest people and you have been wronged. If you sign this you will be repaid for your damages over there by the Washita."

Will thought the young man looked sincere enough.

"I don't sign government papers," said Mr. Johns.

"Uncle Sam's been real good to you, hasn't he?" Just your 'John Henry' is all you need."

A week later, Mr. Johns returned a check the agent mailed to him, knowing that to cash it would legally turn his land over to the oil men.

The riders on their shadowy horses arrived like the wind. Will heard the horses out in the trees and wondered if the agents were stalking the house around the boundaries.

There were more men than usual. There were even a few older gray-haired men, those who wanted to go back to the old ways. They were talking about dangers and people missing from their lands and homes. They sat at the table with an open map of Indian lands, and when the door crashed open one of them hurriedly tried to fold it away.

Will went pale with that crashing and there were demons of terror in him when Betty Colbert rushed in. She was in a terrible state. Josie, about to offer her some coffee, backed off when she saw how Betty's face had darkened, how her hair was wild and her eyes furious.

Betty was breathing like a runner. "You men tell us we're in danger and don't tell us anything else that's going on and then you go off at night leaving us alone with just a gun. To shoot who, I want to know?"

Will was already in the room. He was drawn in by the angry power of this woman whose voice came from the house of wind up in the hills.

Mr. Johns said, "Your house is protected, Miss Colbert. My older boys probably followed you here to make certain you are safe."

And though he was carried into it, Will had a feeling beneath his heart that he wanted to cry. His brothers were not helping uncles after all but were out there at the edge of the clearing, watchers in the dark, hidden from the thin lights of houses.

"This didn't used to be such a hard country," Betty Colbert said. She sat down, almost in tears. "Then they go and cut down all the timber and the young people disappear when they get old enough to sign over their land, like Mr. Clair's son showing up in England with those oil men. Kidnapped all the way to England. Then the best land is turned to oil so we can't even feed the animals or us."

So the women went to work too and Josie sat up alternate nights with Will out on the porch, hiding the pistol in the folds of her skirt while James was riding patrol. But here and there a body would turn up, in the lake or hidden beneath leaves the wind blew away.

In the white fire of noon, the air slowed. It was a beautiful summer day and in the light there were no hints of any danger.

Will's brothers had gone to the rodeo where they rode bareback broncs and roped cattle to earn extra cash. Last year Dwight paid a two dollar entry fee and won the $40 bull-riding purse. Ben lost more money than he made gambling on the horse races and he accused the horses of being cursed and went to pick up the dirt from their tracks, while the white men called him a "Crazy Indian." But he had known all the horses and each one's flair for speed and sure enough in the shadows of the horses, he found lizards with new green tails. He threw back his shoulders: "You whites are all fixers."

Will thought of this as he stood beside Shorty, the black horse. He thought how Shorty was like silver and not a skittish bone in his body. He'd ride that beautiful black horse to the rodeo and sit straight like his father and be proud of the way his shirt sleeves billowed in the wind. He'd keep the mighty energy of the horse reined in just enough to pull back the wide strong neck like a show horse.

He put the bit in its mouth, a red wool blanket on the back of the horse, and led him outside the fence. The horse was quiet and passive even after Will's weight was on him. "Gittup!" Will hit him with his heels and tightened his knees.

The black horse stood there a moment, then he was like a fire going through straw, burning and moving all at once. He turned in circles while Will leaned forward to hold on, his legs without stirrups unable to hold the horse's body.

It was a delirious sparring match for the black horse, raised to be invisible in the dark, trained to James Johns' body, hypnotized by words to know all the stories of humans, even those of a boy's pride and vanity.

Will tried to run Shorty into the trees to slow him down but the black horse cut a tight corner and veered off again before Will could leap down or grab a branch. The branches slapped at Will until he was forced to bury his face deep into the black mane and wait for the horse to tire, but Lord, the entire earth would be threadbare before one muscle on that animal wore out, and Will tasted blood on his lips. The horse was the wind or a river and Will was only a leaf on its current.

Will didn't know how long his father had watched before riding up alongside Shorty and stopping the wild horse from his dance of fire. Shorty's fur was damp and smelling like hay and Will and the red blanket slid down.

"I told you, stay away from that horse," said Mr. Johns and he whipped a leather strap against Will's leg while Shorty snorted and whinnied and stamped the ground like he was laughing.

Later, the rodeo still going, Will sat over his schoolbook and thought what his act might have cost. He hadn't known his father was guarding their house in the daylight or that the Willis house had been dynamited the night before.

It was not so much that Will was down at the heels about missing the rodeo or being humiliated by that horse as that he was learning too young about fear and hatred. The Indians thereabouts had just begun to learn not to trust the agents. They were slow to understand that white people spoke words they don't mean when they want land or money, that when they said life, what they meant is death. The more Indians that began to understand this, the more deaths there were. The gods had lost their ways and all Will knew was that the midnight cries of birds terrified him and he woke sweating in the night when the riders passed by.

It was an unseasonably cool year and the pasture was not rich and green, so one morning Mr. Johns woke the boys early to drive their uncle's cattle and their own few head to a better pasture.

They'd been under surveillance by the Uncle Sam officers, especially now that Dwight was about to turn the age when he could sign over the lands the oil company already held down by the river valley, so Ben and Josie remained at the place with an uncle while Will rode along with the heavy plodding cattle.

Will looked tired with dark circles under his eyes. In the saddle he was slumped as if he were sleeping in the few warm rays of sun. They rode past the Hasting's place and he thought about the old woman sitting in the hospital wrapped in a shawl of hope.

All the deaths had taken their toll on everyone. Mr. Johns had been thinking of moving the family out and letting the agents and crooks and leasers have all the allotment land, but each night when darkness fell, after he vowed to himself that they would leave, he found himself again saddling Shorty or sitting at the door listening for strangers. And Josie said she wouldn't leave any place again and what would become of the boys moving on all the time to escape the Uncle Sam agents.

James Johns rode up alongside Will and touched the side of the boy's knee. He felt amazed at the life and warmth of him. Will felt a promise in the heavy hand.

"Son, I was just wondering if you'd like to ride Shorty."

That damn horse laughed. Will saw it. That horse laughed, and the cattle moved a little quicker toward the pasture and the clouds brightened and there were flowers in the fields.

# INTRODUCTION

## *Amen*

The timing of this story is post-Depression. For most Southern Oklahoma Indians, the Depression was another tragic event following a hundred years of loss and removal. What happened in Oklahoma was planned poverty, with the banks loaning Indian people money for food, seed, and survival, when the bankers knew they could foreclose on the Indian farmers and ranchers who did not have the slightest chance of paying back the loans.

My family, like most Chickasaws, had managed to accumulate horses and cattle, but lost them all during this time. That is why we are now landless and sometimes a broken people.

This was ten years before I was born, but the loss and pain of that time were so great that stories of the Depression became embedded deep inside me and it was as if I had lived through those times. Those times told us once again that we were still Indian and that the land belonged to Others; that we could be moved always from territory to territory.

At least on the surface, Chickasaws had conformed, with a veneer of Christianity that shone across the old ways, that appearance of the southern farmer in the broken hands and nails and missing fingers of the men, the taking on of many traits of the dominant culture only to discard them in private. My grandparents, when I knew them, seemed mighty Indian to me except for the fact that my grandmother played the violin, an ability I didn't associate with tribal people. But they were pretty quiet about being Indians until I thought about the meaning of the words on their tombstones: "Born and died in Berwyn Indian Territory." They had not acknowledged statehood. They resisted, and it was a strong and significant act.

It is into this time that Sullie walks. Sullie is a beloved part of myself. The rural part. The Oklahoma part. She is who I might have been if my life hadn't veered off this way and that; to Denver, to Germany, to Oregon. She's who I could have been if I'd remained with one community, with security, love, judgement, and wonderful gossip. She would have, even at that, hungered to go off to Denver, Germany, and Oregon. Even as a character, she would eventually leave.

Jack is a composite of my grandfather and his brothers. Like my grandfather, Jack really *is* related to the James boys. Our family name is Henderson and some of us Hendersons were pallbearers for Jesse James, just like the story says. And it's part of why we're so damned mean, we joke. It's in our blood.

My great grandfather was white. Three years ago, a family friend named Pud Bean told me and my dad how my great grandfather Young was so land hungry that he used to hire killings. He was like many of the white men who married Indian women in the Territory, especially after Oklahoma was discovered to be rich in oil. He was responsible for that 38¢ death.

This story is so much our history: the cotton that grew too high but never produced, the dead mules, the losses, the survival of traditional land values in the face of Christianity and mixed blood, the absolute crimes of woman-beating and dishonesty, and my great uncle Willy who really did wear a size 2 Brogan, as Pud Bean called those shoes.

In real life the fish in this story was a catfish, but how I wanted those scales like mica in this story. Everybody knows you skin a catfish, so I had to change the main character, just as I changed the location. This lake is Lake Murray just outside of Ardmore where we camp each time we go to a family feast. We camp there with my Aunt Thelma who used to be a great basketball player at Indian school, who later taught at Chilloco, and married David who also taught there. I like that lake. My father helped do the stonework around it when he was with the CCC during the Depression. It has warm water at night. I've been in it so I know.

My father says there is no such thing as an Indian fish, as far as the names of fish go, although there are buffalo fish. But that fish, it's an Indian fish. It brings the people together. It makes a story. It pulls the life out of all events and revitalizes the people. It's huge and it means survival. Even if it seems gone, it is just transformed into the life of the people, and whether there are names or not, we know who we are.

# AMEN

He was born with only one eye and maybe that's why he saw things different than most people. The good eye was dark. The sightless eye was all white and lightly veined.

"There's a god in the light of that eye," Sullie's mother said.

Sullie only saw the man's eye once in her life. It was the night of the big fish and she thought it was more like a pearl or moon than like an eye. And it was all the more unusual because Jack was, after all, only an ordinary man. He had an old man's odor and wasn't always clean.

He carved wood and fished like all the men. With his small hands he carved tree limbs into gentle cats, sleeping dogs, and chickens. And he carved chains to hold them all together.

"It's the only way I can keep a cat and dog in the same room," he joked.

Sullie kept most of his carvings. She watched the shavings pile up on the creaking porch until a breeze blew them into the tall grass or weeds. On a hot windless day they'd fall onto the gold back of the sleeping dog or on its twitching ear. She sat at old Jack's feet and watched and smelled the turpentine odor of wood. His unpatched eye was sharp and black. She could see herself in it, her long skinny legs folded under, her faded dress, dark scraggly hair, all in his one good eye. The other eye was covered, as usual, with a leather patch.

Even then he had been pretty old. His skin was loosening from the bones. He was watching with his clear and black eye how the sky grew to be made of shadows. And some days he didn't have room for one more word so they sat in silence.

The night of the big fish, people had been talking about Jack. He wasn't at the picnic and that was as good invitation to gossip.

"Jesse James was part Chickasaw," said Enoch. "Pete has one of his pistols. Word has it that Pete and Jack are related to the James brothers."

Gladys waved her hand impatiently. She leaned her chair back a little and stuck her chest out. "Go on. That old man?"

"That old man was a pallbearer at Jesses Jame's funeral, yessir."

"They wouldn't have had an Indian at the funeral, would they?" she asked.

"Look it up. Besides, in his younger days he wore a coal black shirt, even when it was hot. And he had one of them there Arabian horses no one else knew how to ride. And a concho belt made out of real silver. Had a silver saddle horn, too."

Will smiled at the other men. He removed his hat and rubbed back his thick black and gray hair. "That's right. Rumor has it his own brother stole that saddle and belt."

People still kept watch for it, for the stirrups dangling like half-moons and the hammered conchos down the sides. There had also been the horsehair bridle he brought back from Mexico. It was red, black and white horsehair with two heavy threads of purple running through it. The purple dye had come from seashells. Greek shellfish, someone said and Jack liked to touch the threads and feel the ocean in them, the white Greek stucco buildings, the blue sky. He liked the purple thread more than all the silver. Almost.

"You wouldn't have crossed him in those days. He won that horse in a contest. The trader said if anyone could ride it, they could have it. Jack got on and rode it. He sure did. And then the trader said he couldn't give it to Jack. 'I'd be broke,' he said. So Jack said, 'Give me fifty dollars.' The man said he didn't have that kind of money. Jack pulled out his pistol and said, 'If I kill you, you won't have no worries about money or horses.'"

Everyone nodded. A couple of old folks said, "Amen," like good Baptists do. A cheater was a bad man. Jack's brother killed a man for cheating him out of thirty-eight cents. It didn't sound like much but there wasn't much food in those days and the thief had been an outsider. The old folks then also said, "Amen." They had to feed their own. Not much grew out of the dry Oklahoma soil except pebbles. Word had it that this was just a thin layer of earth over big stone underground mountains. Close to the hot sun and the corn-eating grasshoppers.

And even Sullie had lived through two droughts, a dozen or more black and turquoise tornadoes roiling through the sky, and the year that ended in October. That year cotton grew up out of the soft red soil and it grew tall. At first the old people praised the cotton and said "Amen" to the ground. But it kept growing until it was tall as the houses, even the houses with little attics. It stretched up to the wooden rooftops, above the silvered dry wood.

Jack went out in the mornings looking for signs of blossoms. Every morning he stood at the far end of the field and sang a song to the cotton. Sullie went out behind him and hid in the tall green plants. She heard parts of the song and silence and the cotton whisper and grow. No pale flowers ever bloomed. No hint of anything that would dry and burst open with white soft cotton inside. Jack went out daily. He stood and sang. He walked through the plants as if his steps would force the stems to let out frail blossoms.

Sullie's mother watched from the door. She dried her hands on the back of her skirt. "I don't think nothing's going to work." She whispered to Sullie and it was true because when October came the taller-than-houses plants froze, turned transparent and then dried a dull yellow. And the banks closed. And the new red mules died of bloat. And Sullie learned to keep silent at the long empty table.

"He even shot his own brother-in-law for beating up his sister. At a picnic just like this one."

"Amen," the women said, good Baptists. They nodded their round dark faces in agreement.

"After that he'd never sit by a window or go in a dark room. Why, he wouldn't even go into a barn unless it had two doors because he was sure the law or someone from the family would get him."

"He was mean, all right, a man to be feared. You'd forget he had such tiny little hands. And he only wore a size two shoe. Don't know how he ran so fast or handled them guns. And all the time turning his head like a rooster to make up for the missing eye."

It grew dark and several men went down to the lake to jack fish. They shined big lights into the water and it attracted fish the same way it paralyzed deer or other land animals. They wouldn't have done it if Jack had been there.

Sullie went down to the water. She was almost a teenager and she liked to watch the big men. She liked their tight jeans and shirts and hats. The women didn't like girls following the men but they forgot about her soon, they were so busy talking about new cotton dresses, their own little children sleeping now on blankets on the hillside. And later they'd talk about women things, men, herbs, seeing Eliza George, the old doctor woman who healed their headaches and helped them get pregnant. Sullie would be back in time to hear about Miss George and how to get pregnant.

But for now she watched the lights shine on the water. And light underneath showing up like sunset. A few miles away in the dark she saw the passing headlights of trucks. She sat in a clump of bushes and trees for a while, then went down to the dark edge of the lake. The men couldn't see into the darkness because of the bright lights in their eyes.

She waded in the warm water. The hem of her dress stuck to her legs. She went a little deeper. She stubbed her toe and felt something move and give way. Whatever it was made a large current and she felt frightened. It was cool and slippery and swam like a large fish. Then it stopped. She reached her hand into the water, wetting even her hair, but it was gone. She felt nothing except the fast motion of water.

She smelled the water. She swam a little and looked at the lights the women kept on the table, and the black trees.

She heard voices of the men out in the center of the lake. "Over there," someone said. And the lights swayed on the water.

Jack walked down to the lake. Sullie started to call to him but then kept still. In the moonlight she saw that he wasn't wearing his eyepatch. And he walked still like maybe he was mad. So she kept silent and waded a little further into rocks and weeds and darkness near the shore.

He didn't have a boat or canoe and he stood a moment at the edge of the dark water. Then he dunked himself and stood again. Sullie saw his knobby shoulders beneath the wet shirt, the bones at the neck. Then he submerged himself in the water and swam toward the other men. There were only a few splashes, an occasional glimpse of his head rising out of the water.

Before he reached the men with lights, Sullie heard them all become noisy at once. "Lordy," one of them said. The water near them grew furious and violent. One small canoe tipped and the lights shone off all directions.

Sullie waded out again to her chest to watch, forgetting about the women's talk. She heard the men's voices. "I could put my hands in that gill slit." Someone else said, "Watch his fins. They're like razor blades." They were pulling something around, taking ropes out of the boats when Jack arrived. Sullie didn't hear the conversation between Jack and the other men but she saw him breathing hard in one of the boats and then he was gone, swimming again toward shore, her direction.

"Pry it out of those rocks," Enoch yelled.

The men were jubilant, dredging up the old fish with only one eye. It was an old presence in the lake and Jack must have known about it all along. His absence had given the younger men permission to fish with illegal light.

He came up from the water close to Sullie and walked through the rocks and sand out into the night air.

Sullie followed Jack a ways. In the darkness there was a tree standing in moonlight, the moon like a silver concho. Jack's hands were small and the light outlined the bones and knuckles. They were spotted like the sides of the ancient fish.

She held herself back from the old man. His shoulders were high and she remembered how he had made cornbread on the day of her birth and fed her honey so she'd never be thin. Sullie's mother had been surprised that Sullie knew this. "Who told you?" she asked.

"Nobody."

"You remember it on your own? Babies can't see."

"I just remember, that's all."

And now he stood breathing in the dark. And there were yucca plants at his feet. After the first freeze they would scatter a circle of black seeds on the earth like magic. Like the flying wisteria seeds that had hit and scared Sullie one night. So much mystery in the world, in the way seeds take to air and mimosa leaves fold in delicate prayer at night.

"Who's there?" he said.

"It's me." Her voice was weak. She was afraid to go near him, afraid to run off. He turned and the sight of his eye made her pull her breath too fast into her lungs. It was bright as the moon and the lanterns on water. He watched her a moment and then turned. He looked toward where the cotton was growing this year, toward a few scattered houses with dark windows. Fireflies appeared while he stood. And the sounds of locusts and crickets Sullie hadn't noticed before.

"Let's go back to the rest of the folks," he said.

And they walked, the skinny wet girl, the skinny wet man. The women shut up when they saw them coming. The men didn't notice. They were dragging the rope-bound old fish up on the shore and all the children were awake and running and splashing the water.

Its fins slowed. The gills quit opening while they cut at it and cleaned it of red and yellow ropey intestines and innards. Dogs lapped at its juices.

In the moonlight the sharp scales were scraped off like hunks of mica in a shining glassy pile.

The smell of fish cooking. The dogs eating parts of the head. So large, that dull-colored thing. They'd all talk about it forever. Something that had survived the drought, the famine, the tornadoes and dead crops. It grew large. It was older than all of them. It had hooks in it and lived.

Sullie refused to eat. She pushed her dish away. Her mother hit the table with a pot. "Eat," she said.

Jack's one eye looked far inside Sullie. She was growing old. She could feel it. In his gaze, she grew old. She grew silent inside. She pulled the plate toward her and looked at the piece of fish, the fried skin and pale bones of it.

"Eat it," Jack motioned with his fork, his own cheeks full of the pink meat. "Eat it. It's an Indian fish."

"Amen," said the women just like they'd always been good Baptists.

# INTRODUCTION

## *Crow*

In 1983 I was in Claremore, Oklahoma, doing poets-in-the-schools. A Cherokee man named Oscar, and his wife Mary, owned a restaurant in town. One night after they closed shop we were talking and Oscar began telling stories. Oscar told me he'd come home to Oklahoma like an elephant, in order to die, but instead of dying, he opened an Italian restaurant.

He told me about his grandmother who had over one hundred grandchildren and none of them came to see her anymore. She kept mints in her pockets. She complained about loneliness. Her grandson or nephew or brother broke the wing of a crow in order to make company for her.

Half a year later I was making a tablecloth with strawberry printed cotton and I loved the material so much I wanted to write a story and put that tablecloth in it. I have an apron like that, too. As soon as I started to write, Oscar's grandmother took shape. I'd almost forgotten her, my life had been so fast that year.

I made the story contemporary. There are never enough stories about who we are now. Besides, that gave me the bumperstickers.

In a way, Grandma is all my family and me. She holds the rich in disdain and envies them at the same time. She knows that good people never have money, but she fears poverty. It is a story about class and race, about our beliefs about ourselves, about getting even with the rich often at our own expense. What have we got to lose? The words Grandma speaks to the rich lady are my Uncle Jake's words and are straight from the border humor between Texas and Oklahoma.

The story of the crow charred black is familiar to most Oklahoma tribes, and the radio sermon also is for real. This is a story about real life and that is important to me. There's love, but it's hidden behind layers of pain, fear, and church-teaching. There's beauty in the people who make up this story, and their beauty radiates out of Chickasaw cornmeal pancakes and the small gestures and events of rural life and those who live it and leave it and remember it.

# CROW

Even though she always has peppermint in her apron pockets, nobody much visits Grandma any more. Once in a while my brother, Buster, stops by to pick me up and we go out to the flats to see her. Or someone who has moved away returns to town on their summer vacation to look over their old homeplace, trying to pick up the lost pieces of their lives, wanting stories about their kin. They stop by to ask my grandmother where old so-and-so has gone. More often than not, she directs them to the cemetery, peppermint candy in their hands.

"That bag goes out to the car." I point at the brown paper sack. Buster moves the coleus plants and the clay sheep that has grass sprouting from its back like green wool. He snoops in the bag. "The cookies are in the cupboard," I tell him.

He opens the cupboard and rummages around for the Oreos. I have just enamelled the kitchen and the cabinet doors stick. "Leave them open," I say to Buster. I inspect the kitchen before leaving for Grandma's. It passes my scrutiny, the clean blue paint and the new tablecloth I made of white strawberry-print cotton.

We pack up Buster's Chevy with my clothes, the groceries, my dog Teddy, and the radio I bought for Grandma. We drive past the Drunkard Brethren Church. There are some people, perhaps the choir, standing outside in dark robes. I think we look pretty flashy, passing by in the gold Chevrolet with shining chrome, and the bumperstickers saying *Indian Affairs are the Best*, and *Pilgrim, Go Home*. I sit very straight with my eyelids lowered even though inside my body I am exhilarated, enjoying this ride in my brother's car. We drive past the stand of scrub oak and then turn off the paved road into the silence that exists between towns. The crows fly up off the road, cursing at us. Since his wife isn't along, Buster accelerates and lets the car go almost as fast as it will, "tying on the tachs." We speed along. "I clocked her at one ten," he says. He slows down by the cornfields, and paces himself on out through the flatlands where Grandma lives. It has been raining and everything is moist and bright, the outlines of the buildings cleaner than usual.

When we pull off the road at Grandma's I stay in the car a few minutes to look at the morning glories she has planted. They are blooming, the blue flowers on a vined arch over the old front door. The Heaven Blue circles nod in the ozone-smelling breeze.

Teddy is anxious to get out and go searching for moles. He whines and paces across the back seat. "Let that damn dog out," Buster says, but he opens the door before I can turn around and get to it. Teddy runs out barking, his tail pulling him sideways with joy. Grandma hears. She comes to the door and stands waiting in the shade, surrounded by the morning glories on her front steps. She already has her hand in her apron pocket, ready to lure us with peppermint, when Teddy turns and circles back viciously, barking at a car that has pulled up silently behind us. I didn't hear the limousine drive up and now Teddy is all around it, barking and raging at the waxed, shining dark metal of the car, and at its tires that remain miraculously clean, even driving through the mud.

"Theodore!" I yell out his proper name, reserved for reprimands and orders. Teddy continues to bark, his golden tail down between his short Dingo legs, his claws digging into the wet red clay. The chauffeur ignores him and goes around stiffly to open the back car door.

Grandma is taking it all in, looking proud and pompous. She respects money but she hates those people who have it. All money is dirty, she has said. It all started with the Rockefellers and their ilk. Now she remains standing very straight and tall, her hand still in the blue-flowered pocket, while a woman is let out of the car and begins walking across the chicken yard. The white woman's shoes are expensive. They are rich beige leather and I feel tense watching her heels dig into the clay soil and the chicken droppings. The muddy clay tries to suck the woman down. The chickens make a path for her, scurrying off and clucking. A copper hen that has been roosting in a tree falls out and screeches, runs off muddy, waddling.

I recognize the lady. She stopped in once for a meal at the Hamburger Heaven where Buster used to work. She was out of place and the customers and employees all stared at her. She made them uneasy and they alternately talked too much and too loud, or they were silent. When the order was ready, Buster took several plates around the room and stopped at the woman's table, flustered. He was overly serious in his discomfort, his face tense. Like an accusation, he said, "You're the hamburger." Laughter floated up into the entire room.

I step out close to hear the conversation between Grandma and the woman. Grandma's jaw is tight like trouble is in the air. While they talk, I pull a stamen from a morning glory and suck it.

"I'd like to buy two dozen eggs," says the beige shoe lady, opening her pocketbook and releasing the odor of French perfume and money.

"We're all out of eggs." Grandma still has her hand in her pocket. She avoids looking at the woman's face. She looks past her at the horizon. It is the way she looks through city people, or people with money, as though they aren't there.

"I'll take a bag of feed then." The woman is thin and wispy. Her hair falls forward as she opens her wallet. The bills are neatly ordered. I can't help but notice Grandma's eyes on them.

"Haven't had any feed delivered from the co-op as late," says Grandma, nonchalantly. Grandma is the local distributor of feed grain and Watkins products, including the cherry-flavored drink mix. She keeps an entire room neatly stocked with bags of grains and bottles of vanilla, aspirin, vitamins, and linament. And she sells eggs. It is how she supports all those chickens, she claims.

Grandma offers the woman a mint, but the woman refuses and grows huffy. "Probably the diet type," I hear Buster say under his breath and I'm sure the woman overheard him because she is clearly put out, and says to Grandma, "Why don't you close all the way down or put a sign out?"

"I'm fixing to once you leave." I can feel a smile under Grandma's words even though her face has no expression and her eyes are blank, staring off into Kansas or some other distant state. The woman doesn't know she is being made fun of, and she wants something else, I can tell. She wants to help Grandma out, to be good to the less fortunate, or something. It is often that way with the rich. But it seems to me that there are some barriers in life that can't be passed through by good deeds or money. Like the time I found a five dollar bill on the floor of the movie theater and felt like a thief for picking it up. It was a fire in my pocket. On the way home I saw a man going through the trash, collecting cans to cash in. I took out the bill and handed it to him. I said I just found it and maybe it was his. He took it, but there was a dreadful and shameful look on his face and I knew then that everyone ought to stay in their own place, wherever that may be, without trespassing on other people's lives. Maybe money just goes where it wants and leaves the rest of us alone.

But Grandma will not be shamed, even though the house looks dilapidated in contrast to the woman and her car. Grandma is proud enough still to plant the flowers and water them with the blue plastic pitcher.

The woman returns to the limousine and they drive away. If it weren't for the recent rain, the car would have covered the morning glories in a cloud of dust. I wonder what it is that made the chaffeur so anxious to leave.

"Last week she wanted to buy the house," Grandma says, and takes out two lint-covered peppermint kisses and gives one each to me and Buster.

"This old place?" Buster has no tact. I give him one of my looks which he has said could kill, but he goes on talking. "How much did she offer you? You should have taken it." His cheek is swollen with peppermint. "You are probably sitting on an oil well."

But Grandma loves her home and will never leave it as long as she lives.

Now and then, she is in a bad mood and this is going to be one of those times. Her eyes are sullen. I remind myself of her better moments. Out loud I say to Buster, "Remember the day we took Grandma to town? When she was in such a good humor that she went up to that tall policeman and asked, 'Do you know where any trouble is?"

Buster's smile begins on the left side of his face, but Grandma ignores what I say. She hands me the egg basket. "Sis, why don't you go out and gather up the eggs?"

Teddy is overjoyed to go with me, looking in the corners of the barn, the storage shed, under old tires on the ground. I find a few eggs in new places, in a batch of damp grass, under the morning glories. Teddy runs in circles and the crows fly up around us. They remind me of stories, like how Old Crow Raven used to be white, white snowy feathers, marble white beak and claws, until one day he got too sure of himself and offered to go to an island of fire and bring back a coal for the two-legged, unwinged people. As he descended to the island, following the orange flames and black smoke billowing up from a hollow tree, he was overcome with the heat and blinded by a thick dark cloud of smoke. Disoriented, he flew straight into the flames and was scorched. That is the reason, people say, why the crows are black. Grandma's theory is that the bird went for the wrong reasons. He didn't really care about the people at all. He just wanted to prove his worth.

When I go inside and set the eggs on the table, Grandma is on one of her lectures about how people are just like blackbirds except they are paling. "Money is turning everybody to white," she says. "All the Indians are going white. Oh, I suppose they still care about their little ones and go to church on Sunday, but all they've got their minds on is the almighty dollar." She stops abruptly while I recount the eggs. There are thirty-one of them, and what with yesterday's eggs around the house, she could have sold the woman four dozen or so. She fixes her gaze on me and the whites around her dark pupils startle me. Even the eggs seem to wobble on the unlevel table. "How come you never come to visit me anymore? I have a hundred grandchildren and no one ever comes out here." It's no use arguing, so I don't answer.

"They're all trying to make a buck, Grandma," Buster says.

Most of the time Grandma doesn't have anyone to talk to and she gets lonely. All of my cousins have been breaking away like spiders, going to cities, to California, marrying and moving. That's why I brought her the radio.

"I don't want to hear anything about money or bucks." Her jaw is tight. She looks straight at Buster.

I turn on the water in the sink and the sound of it running drowns out Grandma's voice. She is still talking about all the Indians out here acting like white people, and about how no one comes to see her. "Those men bullying their sons," she says. "They shoot the birds right out of the air. And money, I wouldn't touch that stuff if you paid me to." And then she notices the radio and becomes quiet. "What's this?"

I dry my hands and plug it in. "I brought it for you. I thought you might like some music." I turn the station selector. Buster says, "You can talk to *that* thing all you want."

I put it on a gospel station, because that is her favorite music. But it's only a man talking and he has a bad voice. *I know my mother went to heaven, harumph, and I had a brother who died and I know he went to heaven.* The man clears his throat. *One by one, we uh, proceed, our candles lighted. We, you, you, I, I think that maybe some of those Europeans haven't reached the heights of Christianity, harumph, that we have, but maybe we have really gone below them and maybe we have, uh, wronged them.*

Buster imitates a rooster, his fists in his armpits. "Bock, Bock," he says. I give him a dirty look.

"Don't you make fun," Grandma says. "The first time I ever heard a radio, don't you know, was Coolidge's inaugural address."

And she starts in again, right over the voice of the radio, about how no one comes to talk to her and how we don't even call her on the telephone. Buster gets angry. He says she's getting senile and he walks out the door and slams it. Grandma and I are silent because he walked out stiff and angry, and the radio says, "*I got saved from the sermons your preach, uh, that's what he said, and from the sermons on your pages in the mail.*"

I'm still thinking about going to heaven with a candle, but I hear Buster outside, scurrying around. I look out the window but can't tell what he's doing.

When he returns, he is carrying a crow and tracking in red mud. "How did you catch that?" I ask. Its eyes are wild but it is beautiful with black feathers shining like silk and velvet. I go closer to look at it. "Can I touch it?" I put my hand over the bird. "Is it hurt?"

Buster pulls back and looks me in the eye. His look scares me. He is too intense and his eyes are darker than usual. He takes hold of the wing. "Don't," I say, but he grabs that glorious coal-colored wing and twists it.

"Buster!" I yell at him and the crow cries out too.

He throws it down on the floor. I'm too afraid to move. "Now, don't say no one comes to see you. That damn crow won't leave. You can tell him all you want how nobody comes to see you." Buster stalks out and we hear the car engine start. I am standing, still unable to move, looking at the bird turning circles on the floor, and beginning to cry. "Oh, Grandma, how could Buster be so awful?" I go down to pick up the injured bird, but it tries to get away. I don't blame it. There's no reason to be trusting. Grandma is sad too, but she just sits at the table and I know we are both thinking of Buster's cruelty and we are women together for the first time.

I turn off the radio and I am thinking of all the poor earthly creatures.

There is a cardboard box in the Watkins room so I go in to get it for the bird and notice that the room is full of the feed Grandma refused to sell the beige shoe lady.

Grandma has already broken a stick and is fitting it to the bird's wing. It is quiet in her hands. I strip off a piece of red calico cotton from her quilting cloth. She takes it in her wrinkled hand and wraps the smooth wing.

"I hate him," I say. "He's always been mean." But Grandma doesn't say anything. She is busy with the crow and has placed it in the box on a nest of paper towels.

"I guess that's what happens to people who think about money all the time," she says. "They forget about the rest of life. They pay no mind to the hurts of each other or the animals. But the Bible teaches me not to judge them." Still, she says nothing else about money or visitors.

The crow listens when Grandma talks. For several days it has been nodding its head at her and following her with its eyes. It listens to the gospel radio, too. "That crow is a heartbreaker," she says. "Just look at him." I hope it isn't true. It is a lovely bird and sometimes it cries out weakly. It has warm black wings and eyes made of stolen corn. I am not a crow reverencer, but I swear that one night I heard it talking to Grandma and it was saying that no one comes to visit.

Grandma is telling it a story about the crows. "They were people and used to speak our tongues," she tells it. It listens. It is raining outside and the rain is hitting the windows. The earth is full of red puddles and they are moving. Somewhere outside, a door is slamming open and closed in the wind.

"You'd like that rain water," she tells the crow. "Make your feathers soft."

Though I am mad at Buster, I can see that he was right. This bird and Grandma are becoming friends. She feeds it grain and corn. It rides on her shoulder and is the color her hair used to be. Crow pulls at the strands of her gray hair. It is like Grandma has shed a skin. She is new and soft, a candlelight inside her.

"Bird bones heal pretty fast," she tells me. "Not like ours."

"Can we listen to something besides gospel for a while?" I ask her. She ignores the question so I go into the bedroom to read a magazine and take a nap. The phone rings and I hear grandmother talking and then the radio goes off and the front door opens and closes. I get up and go out into the kitchen but it is silent, except for the bird picking at the cardboard box.

For a moment I consider putting him out in the rain, splint and all, he looks so forlorn. But Grandma would never forgive me. I ask him, "Have you heard that money is evil?"

Teddy is barking at the front door. It's Buster. Even the dog is unkind to him, growling back in his throat. Buster wants to see if we need anything or if I am ready to go home. I don't speak to him and he sits down on the sofa to read the paper. I stay in the kitchen with Crow.

A house without its tenant is a strange place. I notice for the first time that without Grandma's presence, the house smells of Vicks and old wool. Her things look strange and messy, even the doilies on the couch and end tables are soiled. The walls are sweating and the plaster is stained. I can see Buster sitting on the sofa reading the paper and I decide to tell him I think he is beyond forgiveness.

"Leave me alone." He stands up. His pants ride low and he puts his hands in his pockets and pushes the pants down lower. It is a gesture of intimidation. "She's got company, hasn't she? And maybe that crow will teach her how to behave." He says he is bringing a cage and I say a cage is no place for a wild bird that longs to be outside in the free air. We are about to get into it when Grandma returns. She is crying. "I ought to kill myself," she says.

We grow quiet and both look down at the floor. I have never seen her cry except at funerals, and I sneak glances up at her now and then while she is crying, until she tells me, "Quit gawking. I just lost all my money."

"Your money?" I am struck stupid. I am surprised. I know she never believed in banks and I thought she didn't believe much in money either. I didn't know she had any. I worry about how much she lost. By her tears, I can tell it wasn't just the egg money.

"I hid it in the umbrella because I was scared of robbers, and I lost it in the rain. When I went back looking for it, it wasn't there." She checks inside the wet umbrella, opening and closing it as if she couldn't believe its absence, running her hand around the spokes. "I forgot I hid it there. I just plain forgot," she wails. "I used to keep it in the cupboard until I heard about the burglars."

There is a circle of water around her on the floor and her face is broken, but she takes two pieces of peppermint from her pocket and absently hands one to each of us, the old habit overpowering grief. "I think I should have sold that woman the eggs."

She has a lot of sorrow bending her back. "I walked up the road as fast as I could, but it was already gone."

She became as quiet as the air between towns. I turn on the radio and it sounds like a funeral with We Shall Gather at the River. Grandma picks up Crow and he seems to leap right to her chest and balance there on one of the old ivory buttons. She reaches into her left pocket and takes out grains of corn.

Grandma's shoes are ruined. She puts them on the stove to dry but they are already curling upward at the toes and the leather soles are coming apart.

"How's your kids, Buster?"

"Pretty good," but he looks glum. He's probably worried about his lost inheritance.

"How's Flora?"

Buster has his ready-made answers. "Well," he drawls, "by the time I met her I knew what happiness was." I chime in, mocking, "But it was too late to do anything about it." I finish the sentence with him. Grandma looks at me, startled, and is silent a moment, and then she begins to laugh.

There's nothing else to do, so I get up. "Grandma, you want some eggs?" I turn on the stove. "I'll cook up some eggs and cornmeal pancakes." I wonder how much money she had hidden away.

"I'm all out of molasses," she says. "Plum out."

"Buster will go to the store and get some. Won't you Buster?"

"In this rain?" But he looks at me and I look stern. "Oh sure, yeah, I'll be right back." And he carefully folds the paper and picks up his keys and goes to the door. He is swallowed up by the blowing torrents of water.

I take Grandma's shoes off the stove and put them by the back door.

"Edna fell down the stairs last night," Grandma says, an explanation of where she has been. "Broke her hip."

"How is she?"

"I didn't get to see her. Because of the money. Maybe Buster will take me."

I put some batter in the pan and it sizzles. Crow chatters back at it and it sounds like he is saying how hard it is to be old. I want to put my hand on Grandma's shoulder, but I don't. Instead I go to the window and look out. Crow's lovers or cousins are bathing in the puddles of rain water, washing under their wings and shaking their feathers. I think Crow is the one who went to that island after fire and now, even though his body is so much like the night sky, he is doomed to live another life. I figure he's going to stay here with Grandma to make up for his past mistakes. I think Grandma is right about almost everything. I feel lonely. I go over and touch her. She clasps my hand tightly and then lets go and pats it. "Your pancakes are burning," she says.